WINTER DRINKS

WINTER DRINKS

Over 75 recipes to warm the spirits including hot drinks,
fortifying toddies, party cocktails and mocktails

RYLAND PETERS & SMALL
LONDON • NEW YORK

Senior Designer Toni Kay
Head of Production
   Patricia Harrington
Art Director Leslie Harrington
Editorial Director Julia Charles
Publisher Cindy Richards
Indexer Hilary Bird

First published in 2020
by Ryland Peters & Small,
20–21 Jockey's Fields,
London WC1R 4BW
and
341 E 116th St,
New York NY 10029

www.rylandpeters.com

10 9 8 7 6 5

Recipe collection compiled by Julia
Charles. Text © Claire Burnet, Julia
Charles, Jason Clark, Linda Collister,
Jesse Estes, Tori Finch, Liz Franklin,
Laura Gladwin, Dan May, Hannah
Miles, Louise Pickford, Ben Reed
and David T. Smith 2020.

Design and photographs © Ryland
Peters & Small 2020. See page 144
for full text and picture credits.

ISBN: 978-1-78879-275-2

Printed and bound in China.

FSC
www.fsc.org

MIX
Paper from
responsible sources
FSC® C106563

Notes

• Both metric and imperial fl oz./
US cups are included. Work with
one set of measurements and do
not alternate between the two within
a recipe. All spoon measurements
given are level: 1 teaspoon = 5 ml;
1 tablespoon = 15 ml.

• Uncooked or partially cooked eggs
should not be served to the elderly
or frail, young children, pregnant
women or those with compromised
immune systems.

• When a recipe calls for citrus zest
or peel, buy unwaxed fruit and wash
well before using. If you can only find
treated fruit, scrub well in warm
soapy water before using.

• To sterilize screw-top jars, preheat
the oven to 160°C/150°C fan/325°F/
Gas 3. Wash the jars and lids in hot
soapy water and rinse but don't dry
them. Remove any rubber seals, put
the jars onto a baking sheet and into
the oven for 10 minutes. Soak the lids
in boiling water for a few minutes.

CONTENTS

INTRODUCTION

Come the colder months our needs and desires change, especially when it comes to sustenance. The fall in temperature and fewer daylight hours usually means more time spent indoors, perhaps reading a book in front of the fire, playing board games, or simply snuggling under a throw on the sofa to watching a movie. Comforting milky drinks that can be cupped in both hands, offer comfort, security and feelings of nostalgia to accompany these simple pleasures. Outdoor activities, such as winter walks in parks, or rambles across the countryside to gaze upon sparkling snow-covered wonderlands mean a hot toddy with a little nip of neat spirit can warm both hands and hearts whilst on the move. Then, before you know it, the holiday season has arrived, bringing with it invitations to a host of events from cookie exchanges to cocktail receptions, ice skating trips to outdoor Christmas markets, and celebratory dinners with family and other loved ones. Social occasions quickly fill up diaries and come your turn to host you may be looking for inspiration beyond the ubiquitous mulled wine and eggnog.

Here, in this collection, you'll find recipes to cater for all these occasions, and more – from indulgent hot chocolates, fragrant mulled wines and ciders, warming toddies, classic cocktails, party sparklers, fruity mocktails, and fun concoctions to fill your festive punch bowl. The methods are easy to follow and require little or no specialist equipment. If you enjoy creamy, foam-topped coffee drinks then a milk frother is a good investment, otherwise a small whisk will do the job almost as well. Heatproof latte and tea glasses with handles make attractive vessels for beverages such as mulls and toddies, or double-walled tumblers that keep their contents hot but remain cool to the touch are also a stylish choice, but a cup or mug will do. Any aspiring home bartender can always use a cocktail shaker, a measuring jigger and a few pieces of classic glassware especially designed for the job, such as old-fashioned, coupe and martini glasses, but often a small wine glass or tumbler can be substituted. Champagne flutes, highballs and wine glasses are always available to hire, so plan ahead and rent what you need for your larger events. Punch bowls make a wonderful focal point on any festive party table, from simple glass to cut crystal, so if you are lucky enough to have one, possibly even a family heirloom, now is the season to get it out and show it off! If not, any large heatproof bowl or jug/pitcher can be used.

We hope you enjoy this seasonal recipe collection and discover new drinks that bring you comfort and joy and fill your home with good cheer this winter.

COMFORTING

❖

hot chocolates & warm milks

INDULGENT HOT CHOCOLATE

Here is a cup of hot chocolate with bells and whistles on. Serve up this deliciously rich drink, topped with whipped cream, chocolate curls, marshmallows and malt balls when you and yours really need an extra special treat.

85 g/3 oz. dark/bittersweet chocolate (70% cocoa solids), chopped

500 ml/2 cups milk

1 teaspoon soft brown sugar, or more to taste

TO SERVE
whipped cream, for topping

1 large handful of mini marshmallows

dark/bittersweet chocolate curls

milk/semisweet chocolate-covered malt balls

SERVES 2

Put the chopped chocolate and 60 ml/4 tablespoons of the milk in a small heavy-based saucepan and warm gently to melt the chocolate into the milk.

Use a small tubular whisk to stir this mixture into a smooth paste and once you are happy that the chocolate has all melted, only then add the rest of the milk and the sugar.

Bring to the boil stirring all the time. The moment it starts to boil, take off the heat and whisk vigorously for a minute until foamy.

Pour your foaming hot chocolate into 2 cups or heatproof glasses, top each with a spoonful of whipped cream, marshmallows, chocolate curls and finally the malt balls. Add more sugar if you feel the drinks need it.

Serve at once with spoons.

HAZELNUT HOT CHOCOLATE

This drink is a must for hazelnut chocolate spread lovers. It is rich and creamy with a hit of warming hazelnut liqueur. Sprinkled with toasted hazelnuts too, this is an utterly nutterly hot chocolate treat and it is equally delicious without the alcohol if you prefer.

100 g/3½ oz. milk/semisweet chocolate, chopped

500 ml/2 cups milk

1 heaped tablespoon chocolate hazelnut spread (such as Nutella)

4–7 tablespoons Frangelico (hazelnut liqueur)

200 ml/generous ¾ cup double/heavy cream, whipped

1 tablespoon finely chopped hazelnuts, toasted

SERVES 2

Place the chopped chocolate in a heatproof bowl over a pan of simmering water and heat gently over a low heat until melted.

Place the milk in a saucepan and bring gently to the boil. Add the melted chocolate and chocolate hazelnut spread to the pan and simmer over low heat, whisking all the time with a small tubular whisk, until the chocolate is combined. Remove from the heat and add the hazelnut liqueur to taste, if using. (Do not do this over the heat as the alcohol will evaporate.)

Pour the hot chocolate into 2 cups or heatproof glasses. Add a spoonful of whipped cream to the top of each serving. Sprinkle with toasted hazelnuts and serve at once.

S'MORES HOT CHOCOLATE

S'mores are a delicious campfire treat – sticky toasted marshmallows and chocolate are sandwiched between crackers/biscuits. Here this nostalgic treat provides the inspiration for a fun hot chocolate. You might benefit from having a chef's blow torch for this recipe to melt the marshmallows, or ideally an open fire!

2 graham crackers or digestive biscuits

100 g/3½ oz. milk/semisweet chocolate, chopped

250 ml/1 cup milk

250 ml/1 cup double/heavy cream

2 giant marshmallows

a chef's blow torch (optional)

SERVES 2

Begin by preparing 2 heatproof glasses. Crush the crackers or biscuits by placing them in a clean plastic bag and bashing them with a rolling pin. Put the crumbs on a plate.

Place the chopped chocolate in a heatproof bowl over a pan of simmering water and heat over a low heat until melted. Carefully dip the rims of each glass into the chocolate and then the chocolate-coated rim of each glass in the crumbs to decorate. Set aside until you are ready to serve.

Spoon the remaining melted chocolate into a saucepan with the milk and cream, and heat over a low heat, whisking all the time with a small tubular whisk. Pour the hot chocolate into the prepared glasses, taking care not to pour the liquid over the chocolate-crumb decoration.

Place each marshmallow on a toasting fork and toast with the blow torch (or over a hob/stovetop gas flame) to caramelize. Take care not to burn the marshmallows. While the marshmallows are still warm, place one on top of each glass and serve at once.

TOFFEE APPLE HOT CHOCOLATE

Eating a toffee apple is such a thrill – biting into the crisp caramel shell and then finding the juicy fruit underneath. This drink is flavoured with caramelized sugar, and you should take the caramel as dark as you dare. Apfelkorn liqueur is a tasty German apple spirit which is very warming, but optional here.

1 dessert apple

freshly squeezed juice of
½ a lemon

1 teaspoon ground cinnamon

100 g/½ cup caster/superfine
sugar

500 ml/2 cups milk

40 g/1½ oz. white chocolate,
chopped

4 tablespoons Apfelkorn
liqueur (optional)

whipped cream, for topping

dulce de leche or caramel
sauce, to drizzle

*2 baking sheets, 1 lined with
baking parchment*

SERVES 2

Preheat the oven to 140°C /fan 130 °C/275°F/Gas mark 1.

Leaving the skin on, cut the apple into thin slices using a sharp knife or a mandoline. Toss the slices in lemon juice to prevent them browning, then dust in a little ground cinnamon. Lay the slices out flat on the unlined baking sheet and bake in the preheated oven for 1–1½ hours, until dried but still slightly soft.

Place the sugar in a saucepan and heat gently over a low heat until melted. Do not stir, but swirl it to ensure that the sugar does not burn. Once the sugar has melted, carefully dip some of the baked apple slices into the caramel – only dipping them in half way. (Use metal tongs and take extreme care as the sugar is very hot and can burn you.) Place the apple slices on the lined baking sheet and leave to dry.

Add the milk to the remaining caramelized sugar in the pan. Do not worry if the sugar solidifies, as it will melt on heating. Simmer over low heat until the sugar dissolves. Add the chocolate and stir until melted. Remove from the heat and add the apfelkorn liqueur, if using (do not return to the heat as it may curdle the milk). Pour the drink into 2 cups or heatproof glasses, top with whipped cream and drizzle with dulce de leche or caramel sauce. Place an apple slice on top of each one and serve at once.

CHAI-SPICED WHITE HOT CHOCOLATE

Masala chai is a popular Indian drink of milky black tea delicately fragranced with spices such as cinnamon and cardamom. The spicing of the tea varies from region to region, and every family's recipe is different. Here creamy white chocolate is melted into milk and perfumed with warming spices along with a hint of rose water to make an exotic variation on a hot chocolate.

12 green cardamom pods

1 teaspoon caster/superfine sugar

1 cinnamon stick

a pinch of freshly grated nutmeg, plus extra to garnish

500 ml/2 cups milk

1 teaspoon rose extract, rose water or rose syrup

100 g/3½ oz. white chocolate, chopped

a pestle and mortar

SERVES 2

Begin by removing the black seeds from 2 of the cardamom pods and grinding them to a fine powder with the sugar using a pestle and mortar.

Place the ground cardamom and remaining pods in a saucepan with the cinnamon stick, nutmeg and milk, and bring to the boil over a low heat. Remove from the heat and leave the spices to infuse for 15–20 minutes, then discard the whole pods and cinnamon stick.

Add your chosen rose flavouring and the chopped white chocolate to the pan and return to a simmer over a low heat, whisking all the time, until the chocolate has melted. Pour into 2 cups or heatproof glasses and serve at once, sprinkled with freshly grated nutmeg.

CHILLI HOT CHOCOLATE

Spicy heat and chocolate may seem a fiery combination, but fear not, this chocolate is not too hot. The spicing helps to give a depth of flavour to the bitter chocolate. If you are feeling brave, you can make extra candied chillies/chiles to serve alongside your hot chocolate, although poaching them in sugar syrup does take away a lot of the heat.

100 g/½ cup caster/superfine sugar

1–5 fresh large red chillies/chiles

200 ml/generous ¾ cup milk

100 ml/⅓ cup double/heavy cream

100 g/3½ oz. dark/bittersweet chilli/chile chocolate, chopped

SERVES 2

Begin by preparing the candied chillies/chiles. Place the sugar in a heavy-based saucepan with 250 ml/1 cup cold water and simmer over medium heat until the sugar has dissolved. Add the chillies/chiles (with their green tops still attached) to the pan and simmer for 15–20 minutes, until they are soft and their skins are slightly translucent. Remove them from the pan with metal tongs (take care as the syrup will be very hot) and set aside. Reserve the poaching syrup.

Place the milk, cream and chopped chocolate in a saucepan and heat over a low heat until the chocolate has melted, whisking all the time.

Finely chop one of the candied chillies/chiles and add a little of it to the pan, together with about 1 tablespoon of the reserved syrup. (How much you add depends on your own taste and the strength of your chillies/chiles. Add a little to start, then taste and add more if you want a more fiery flavour.)

Pour the hot chocolate into 2 cups or heatproof glasses with saucers and serve at once with extra candied chillies/chiles on the side, if you wish.

CINNAMON & CLEMENTINE HOT CHOCOLATE

⊷⊶

Here very dark/bittersweet chocolate is enriched with a delicious homemade clementine syrup, an aroma that instantly transports many of us to Christmases past. If you have a surfeit of clementines, double the syrup quantity and it will keep in a screw-top jar in the fridge for up to 2 weeks. You can use it, topped up with Prosecco or Champagne, to make a festive cocktail.

1 teaspoon ground cinnamon

500 ml/2 cups milk

100 g/3½ oz. dark/bittersweet chocolate (85% cocoa solids), chopped

about 10 mini marshmallows

unsweetened powdered chocolate or cocoa, for dusting

2 long cinnamon sticks, to serve (optional)

FOR THE CLEMENTINE SYRUP

2 tablespoons caster/superfine sugar

grated zest and freshly squeezed juice of 2 clementines

SERVES 2

Begin by making the Clementine Syrup. Place the sugar and clementine zest and juice in a small saucepan and simmer over a low heat until the sugar has dissolved and the liquid is syrupy. Let cool slightly.

Sleve/strain the cooled syrup into a clean saucepan and add the ground cinnamon, along with the milk and chopped chocolate. Simmer over a low heat until the chocolate has melted, whisking with a small tubular whisk to incorporate the chocolate and froth the milk.

Pour the hot chocolate into 2 cups or heatproof glasses and top with a layer of mini marshmallows. Dust with powdered chocolate and place a cinnamon stick in each glass to act as a stirrer, if using. Serve immediately.

GINGERBREAD HOT CHOCOLATE

Infused with stem ginger and gingerbread syrup, this is the perfect drink to sip by the fireside. If you do not have gingerbread syrup, simply double the quantity of ginger syrup used from the stem/candied ginger jar, and add a little ground cinnamon and a pinch of freshly grated nutmeg to the milk to replicate that trademark spiced gingerbread flavour. For an extra treat, why not serve with gingerbread cookies on the side?

100 g/3½ oz. milk/semisweet chocolate, chopped

500 ml/2 cups milk

1 ball of stem/candied ginger from a jar, chopped

1 tablespoon ginger syrup from the stem/candied ginger jar

1 tablespoon gingerbread syrup, such as Monin (optional, see recipe intro)

whipped cream, for topping

gingerbread man sprinkles (as pictured) or similar, to decorate

SERVES 2

Place the chopped chocolate in a saucepan with the milk, chopped stem/candied ginger, ginger syrup and gingerbread syrup, if using. Simmer over a low heat until the chocolate has melted, whisking all the time with a small tubular whisk.

Remove the stem ginger pieces and discard. Pour the hot chocolate into 2 cups or heatproof glasses and top with plenty of whipped cream. Decorate with gingerbread man (or other) sprinkles, and serve at once.

PUMPKIN SPICE LATTE

Here is a drink that embraces the passion for all things pumpkin come Halloween and Thanksgiving, when everything from pumpkin pie and pumpkin pancake mix and even pumpkin spice peanut butter hit the stores! This drink is easy to make and the perfect beverage to serve at your own seasonal celebrations.

2 tablespoons canned pumpkin purée (such as Libby's)

100 g/3½ oz. white chocolate, chopped

500 ml/2 cups milk

a pinch of freshly grated nutmeg, plus extra to garnish

1 teaspoon ground cinnamon

½ teaspoon ground ginger

1 teaspoon vanilla extract

whipped cream, for topping

a blender (optional)

SERVES 2

Place the pumpkin purée and chopped white chocolate in a saucepan with the milk, nutmeg, cinnamon, ginger and vanilla. Simmer over a low heat until the chocolate has melted, whisking all the time.

For an extra-smooth hot chocolate, place the mixture in the cup of a blender now and blitz for a few seconds. This is optional though, as the drink can also be enjoyed with the slight texture of the purée.

Return the hot chocolate to the pan if necessary, and heat again, then pour into 2 cups or heatproof glasses. Top with whipped cream and finish with an extra grating of nutmeg. Serve at once.

VANILLA & MAPLE SOYACCINO

For those who are lactose intolerant, or have given up dairy as part of a vegan lifestyle, soya/soy milk is the perfect way of still enjoying milky hot drinks. It has a satisfyingly nutty taste but the flavour can vary between brands, so take the time to find one that you like and stick with it!

500 ml/2 cups soya/soy milk

1 teaspoon vanilla extract

4 teaspoons pure maple syrup

ground cinnamon or powdered drinking chocolate, to serve

a milk frother (optional)

SERVES 2

Put the soya/soy milk, vanilla extract and maple syrup in a saucepan and set over a low heat. Warm until it just reaches boiling point.

Remove the pan from the heat and then froth the milk, using a milk frother or whisk vigorously with a small tubular whisk until light and foamy.

Pour the drink into 2 cups or heatproof glasses, dust with ground cinnamon or powdered drinking chocolate and serve at once.

BABYCCINO

These scaled-down mini drinks are fun for small children who want to mimic their parents with a coffee shop-style drink. Of course these are made without coffee but they look just like the real thing, only smaller.

250 ml/1 cup milk

2 teaspoons chocolate syrup or sauce

powdered drinking chocolate, to dust

mini marshmallows, to serve (optional)

a milk frother (optional)

SERVES 2

Put the milk in a saucepan and heat gently until warm, but not hot, then froth the milk using a milk frother or whisk vigorously with a small tubular whisk until light and foamy.

Drizzle a little chocolate syrup or sauce inside 2 small heatproof glasses (to look like dark coffee) and spoon over the frothed milk. Dust with a little powdered drinking chocolate, top with a few mini marshmallows, if using, and serve at once, with little spoons for digging out the chocolate sauce.

GOLDEN SAFFRON MILK

This drink is aromatic and exotic. The saffron, with its earthy flavour and striking golden colour, is pretty as well as delicious and it makes a good bedtime drink. The condensed milk does make this drink very sweet so, if you prefer, reduce the amount used and increase the quantity of milk.

415 ml/1¾ cups milk

60 ml/¼ cup sweetened condensed milk

¼ teaspoon saffron threads, plus extra to serve

3 green cardamom pods, lightly crushed

SERVES 2

Put the milk, condensed milk, saffron threads and cardamom pods in a saucepan and heat gently, stirring constantly, until the mixture just reaches boiling point. Remove from the heat and let the flavours infuse for 5 minutes.

Sieve/strain the milk into 2 cups or heatproof glasses, sprinkle with a few saffron threads and serve at once.

SPICED COCONUT MILK

Coconut brings a delicate flavour and wonderful creaminess to this dairy-free drink. The slight hint of chilli/chile spice adds welcome warmth.

500 ml/2 cups coconut milk

1½ tablespoons soft brown sugar

2 star anise, lightly crushed

1 small red chilli/chile, halved lengthways and deseeded

125 ml/½ cup coconut whipping cream, chilled overnight

toasted shredded coconut, to serve

SERVES 2

Put the coconut milk, sugar, star anise and chilli/chile in a saucepan and set over a low heat. Heat gently for 10 minutes then bring just to boiling point. Strain through a small sieve/strainer into 2 cups or heatproof glasses.

Whip the chilled coconut whipping cream vigorously with a small tubular whisk until it holds its shape and spoon over the drinks.

Sprinkle with a little toasted coconut to garnish and serve at once.

HONEYED MILK WITH RAISINS

All the festive flavours of a British spiced fruit mince pie in a cup – yummy. The star decoration on top is magical, but optional, the drink tastes great either way.

500 ml/2 cups milk

2 tablespoons raisins

1 tablespoon chopped crystallized/candied ginger

2 teaspoons runny honey

2 orange slices

whipped cream, for topping

cinnamon sugar, to dust

a piece of card and a star-shaped pastry cutter, about 5-cm/ 2 inches in diameter (optional)

SERVES 2

Using the pastry cutter as a template, carefully draw a star on the card. Use scissors to cut out the star shape to create a stencil. Set aside until needed.

Put the milk, raisins, ginger, honey and orange slices in a saucepan. Heat gently until it just reaches boiling point. Remove the orange slices and divide the drink between 2 wide-rimmed cups. Spoon some whipped cream over the top of each one.

Hold the stencil over a drink, making sure that the star shape is in the centre. Lightly dust with cinnamon sugar and remove the stencil to leave a star decoration on top. Repeat with the other drink. Alternatively, just dust the surfaces lightly with cinnamon sugar. Serve at once.

WHITE CHRISTMAS

This is a delicious holiday drink bursting with all the evocative aromas of the season, such as orange zest, cloves, cinnamon and nutmeg and a little splash of warming orange liqueur. It's great to serve at the end of a dinner party in place of a heavy dessert, so this recipe serves 6 to allow for that.

1 litre/4 cups milk

200 g/7 oz. white chocolate, grated

2 large pieces of orange zest

4 cloves, lightly crushed

2 cinnamon sticks, lightly crushed

a pinch of freshly grated nutmeg

90 ml/⅓ cup Cointreau or any other orange-flavoured liqueur

125 ml/½ cup double/heavy cream, whipped until stiff

candied orange peel and grated white chocolate, to serve

a milk frother (optional)

SERVES 6

Put the milk, chocolate, orange zests, cloves, cinnamon sticks and nutmeg in a heavy-based saucepan and heat gently, stirring, until it just reaches boiling point. Froth the milk using a milk frother, or whisk vigorously with a small tubular whisk until light and foamy.

Add 15 ml/1 tablespoon of the Cointreau to each of 6 small cups or heatproof glasses. Divide the milk equally among the glasses and spoon a little of the whipped cream on top of each drink. Sprinkle with candied orange peel and grated white chocolate. Serve at once with small spoons.

ROSEMARY MILK

Rosemary may seem an unusual addition to a milky drink but not only is the aroma and flavour wonderful, rosemary has many health benefits too. It has long been known to soothe upset stomachs, aid digestion and help prevent headaches, so perhaps the perfect antidote to a little seasonal over indulgence. Honey is the best way to sweeten this drink, and Greek pine honey, with it's spiced overtones, works particularly well, if you can source it.

500 ml/2 cups milk

2 large fresh rosemary sprigs, washed

1–2 teaspoons runny honey, to taste

SERVES 2

Put the milk in a saucepan. Crush the rosemary sprigs firmly with the flat of a large palette knife and drop them into the pan.

Heat the milk very gently over a low heat until it just reaches boiling point. Remove from the heat and let it sit so that the rosemary can infuse for 5 minutes as it cools.

Sieve/strain the milk, discarding the rosemary, and pour into 2 heatproof glasses or cups, add honey to taste, stir and serve at once.

INVIGORATING

coffee drinks & teas

MOCHACCINO

Strong espresso coffee is combined here with real rather than powdered chocolate to make a delicious and rich-tasting, creamy mocha drink.

50 g/2 oz. dark/bittersweet chocolate, grated

2 shots freshly brewed hot espresso coffee

250 ml/1 cup milk

125 ml/½ cup whipping cream, whipped

a few chocolate-coated coffee beans and grated dark/ bittersweet chocolate, to garnish

a milk frother (optional)

SERVES 2

Put the chocolate in 2 small cups or heatproof glasses and pour a shot of hot espresso coffee into each one. Stir well until the chocolate has completely melted.

Meanwhile, heat the milk in a small saucepan until hot then use a milk frother or a small tubular whisk and beat vigorously until foamy and light.

Pour the milk over the coffee and top with the whipped cream, a few chocolate-coated coffee beans and a sprinkle of grated chocolate. Serve at once.

VANILLA COFFEE

25–30 g/1 oz. (5 level tablespoons) freshly roasted coffee beans

2 vanilla pods/beans, chopped

milk and sugar, to taste (optional)

a coffee grinder

a screw-top jar for storage

MAKES ABOUT 4 SERVINGS

Grinding freshly roasted coffee beans with vanilla pods/beans produces a lovely coffee with a natural aroma and taste. Once ground, use at once or keep in a screw-top jar until ready to use. As a general guideline allow 1-2 tablespoons of ground coffee for every 175 ml/6 oz. of water.

Put the coffee beans and vanilla pods in a coffee grinder and grind finely. Use this mixture to make coffee in your preferred method, adding milk and/or sugar to taste.

CINNAMON COFFEE

25–30 g/1 oz. (5 level tablespoons) freshly roasted coffee beans

1 cinnamon stick or ½ tablespoon ground cinnamon, as preferred

a coffee grinder

a screw-top jar for storage

MAKES ABOUT 4 SERVINGS

This method means you can achieve a hint of cinnamon in your coffee without the need to add a sugary syrup or suffer ground cinnamon clumping together on top of your drink...

Put the coffee beans and cinnamon stick or ground cinnamon in a coffee grinder and grind finely. Use this mixture to make coffee in your preferred method, adding milk and/or sugar to taste.

MOCHA MAPLE COFFEE

Coffee and chocolate make perfect partners as this delicious drink proves. The addition of a sweet, maple-flavoured cream float and an optional chocolate liqueur, makes this the perfect after-dinner drink.

125 ml/½ cup whipping cream

1 teaspoon pure maple syrup

500 ml/2 cups freshly brewed hot coffee (Americano/long black)

2 shots crème de cacao (chocolate liqueur) or chocolate syrup

grated dark/bittersweet chocolate, to garnish

SERVES 2

Lightly whisk the whipping cream and maple syrup together using a small tubular whisk, until the mixture is foamy and has thickened slightly.

Pour the freshly brewed coffee into 2 heatproof glasses or cups and add a shot of crème de cacao or chocolate syrup to each one, as preferred.

Slowly layer the maple cream over the surface of the coffees using a flat-bottomed spoon – this method will help it to 'float' on the surface of the drink. Sprinkle with grated chocolate and serve at once.

IRISH COFFEE

The Buena Vista Cafe in San Francisco is credited with introducing the Irish Coffee to the USA in 1952. Stanton Delaplane, a travel writer, is said to have tasted the drink while in transit at Shannon airport, Ireland. Back in the US, he worked with the Buena Vista Cafe to recreate it. With painstaking effort put into getting the cream to float cleanly on top, they soon realized that adding sugar was the key. Stanton helped to popularize the drink by mentioning it frequently in his travel column.

75 ml/⅓ cup good quality double/ heavy cream

1 sugar cube or 1 teaspoon white sugar

45 ml/1½ oz. Irish whiskey

150 ml/⅔ cup freshly brewed hot espresso coffee (Americano/long black)

freshly grated nutmeg, to garnish (optional)

SERVES 1

Preheat a heatproof goblet glass with hot water and pour the water from the glass.

Shake the cream in a cocktail shaker (or whisk with a small tubular whisk) to a thicker but still fluid consistency.

Put all the remaining ingredients in the warm glass (sugar, whiskey, then coffee), making sure the sugar has dissolved and been stirred into the coffee and whiskey before gently layering the cream over the surface of the drink using a flat-bottomed spoon.

Garnish with grated nutmeg, if using, and serve at once.

DUTCH COFFEE

This simple yet fun play on an Irish Coffee uses Dutch flavours of aged genever, Speculaas cinnamon biscuit/cookie liqueur, Dutch-style cold drip coffee and nutmeg, an ingredient that was once upon a time valued higher than gold by the famous Dutch East India company.

45 ml/1½ oz. aged genever

15 ml/½ oz. Speculaas (cinnamon biscuit/cookie liqueur)

60 ml/2 oz. cold-drip coffee

a dash of cacao bitters

60 ml/2 oz. butterscotch cream (see below)

FOR THE BUTTERSCOTCH CREAM (MAKES 3 SERVINGS)

270 ml/9 oz. whipping cream

15 ml/½ oz. butterscotch liqueur

TO GARNISH

grated dark/bittersweet chocolate

freshly grated nutmeg

a stroopwafel (optional)

SERVES 1

Preheat a heatproof stemmed glass by filling it with hot water. Balance the stroopwafel, if using, on top so it begins to soften from the steam.

For the Butterscotch Cream, put the cream in a squeezy bottle and add the butterscotch liqueur. Shake to thicken. (Or, alternatively, whisk in a bowl with a balloon whisk.)

To make the cocktail, warm the genever, Speculaas liqueur, coffee and cacao bitters in a small saucepan set over a low heat, until just before boiling point. (Or, combine everything in a Boston glass and heat using a coffee machine's steam wand, until just before boiling point.)

To serve, empty the water from the stemmed glass and pour in the cocktail. Layer with the Butterscotch Cream and garnish with grated chocolate and nutmeg. Place the stroopwafel, if using, on top to continue softening, then serve at once.

CAMPFIRE MOCHA

You can pre-batch two or more serves of this fun interpretation of a hot chocolate in a bottle, as it's great to share with friends around a campfire. Naturally it works well made in the comfort of your kitchen too, but it tastes best under a starry sky with campfire smoke in your eyes. To do this, simply add all the ingredients to a bottle, shake then pour into a saucepan set over the flames. Once hot, whisk with a fork and pour into camping mugs. Serve topped with giant toasted marshmallows.

400 ml/1¾ cups milk

90 ml/3 oz. Canadian whisky

2 tablespoons unsweetened powdered drinking chocolate or cocoa

30 ml/2 tablespoons pure maple syrup

80 ml/2¾ oz. cold-brew black coffee

2 giant marshmallows, to garnish

a chef's blow torch (optional)

SERVES 2

Combine the milk, whisky, powdered drinking chocolate, maple syrup and coffee in a saucepan set over a low heat and warm until just below boiling point, whisking continuously with a small tubular whisk. Pour into 2 heatproof glasses or cups.

Place each marshmallow on a toasting fork and toast with the blow torch (or over a hob/stovetop gas flame) to caramelize. Take care not to burn the marshmallows.

While the marshmallows are still warm, place 1 on top of each drink and serve at once.

EGGNOG LATTE

This warming drink with a hint of coffee makes a stimulating alternative to the more traditional eggnog. For a non-alcoholic version, omit the rum.

500 ml/2 cups milk

1 vanilla pod/bean, split

2 very fresh eggs

2–3 tablespoons caster/superfine sugar, to taste

½ teaspoon ground cinnamon

a pinch of freshly grated nutmeg

2 tablespoons dark rum (optional)

250 ml/1 cup freshly brewed hot coffee (Americano/long black)

SERVES 4

Put the milk and vanilla pod/bean in a saucepan and heat gently until the milk just reaches boiling point. Meanwhile, put the eggs, sugar and spices in a bowl and whisk with a fork until frothy. Stir in the milk, then return the mixture to the pan.

Heat gently for 2–3 minutes, stirring constantly with a wooden spoon, until the mixture thickens slightly.

Remove from the heat and stir in the rum, if using, and coffee. Pour into 4 heatproof glasses or cups and serve at once.

CARIBBEAN CAFÉ WITH RUM & MALIBU

This tropical coffee is similar to an Irish coffee (see page 50), where the alcohol and coffee are combined in a glass then lightly whipped cream is carefully poured on top over the back of a spoon so it floats on the surface. Traditionally you then drink the coffee through the layer of frothy cream.

2–4 teaspoons caster/superfine, or granulated sugar, to taste

2 tablespoons dark rum

2 tablespoons Malibu (coconut-flavoured rum liqueur)

250 ml/1 cup freshly brewed hot coffee (Americano/long black)

80 ml/⅓ cup whipping cream

SERVES 2

Divide the sugar, rum, Malibu and coffee between 2 heatproof glasses or cups and stir well. Put the cream in a bowl and vigorously whisk with a small tubular whisk or balloon whisk until foaming and frothy.

Slowly layer the whipped cream over the surface of each coffee, using a flat-bottomed spoon to help it to float. Serve at once.

CATALAN COFFEE PUNCH

This is a traditional hot coffee and rum drink from the Catalonia region of Spain. The alcohol is burnt off before the coffee is added. It is traditional to use a terracotta cooking vessel for this, but a stainless-steel saucepan will work just as well. Be very careful when igniting the rum. Use an extra-long match or a taper to keep your hands well away from the flame.

250 ml/1 cup white rum, such as Bacardi

1–2 tablespoons caster/superfine or granulated sugar

1 cinnamon stick

2 strips of lemon peel

500 ml/2 cups freshly brewed hot coffee

SERVES 6

Put the rum, sugar, cinnamon and lemon peels in a terracotta pot (or other flameproof dish) or a saucepan and stir until the sugar has dissolved.

Very carefully ignite the mixture. Let the flame die down completely then slowly pour in the hot coffee.

Divide between heavy-based and heatproof shot glasses (or demitasse coffee cups) and serve at once.

ESPRESSO MARTINI

Coffee cocktails are now very much a thing, and so they should be – they are absolutely delicious. Leading the charge is the Espresso Martini – although not a new idea it's only really found mainstream popularity in recent years and is now on every cocktail menu. Serve it after a heavy dinner when energy levels are flagging and a 'second wind' is required. Just a few sips with a sugary petit four ensures hitting the dance floor remains an option! This recipe makes 1 classic serve or 2–3 popular mini-serve cocktails, as pictured.

50 ml/2 oz. freshly made strong espresso coffee

50 ml/2 oz. vodka

50 ml/2 oz. coffee liqueur, such as Kahlua or Tia Maria

½ tablespoon pure cane sugar syrup or Simple Sugar Syrup (see note and below)

ice cubes

coffee beans, to garnish (optional)

FOR THE SIMPLE SUGAR SYRUP

300 g/1½ cups caster/superfine or white granulated sugar

150 ml/²⁄₃ cup cold water

a sterilized screw-top jar

SERVES 1-3

Pour all the ingredients into a cocktail shaker filled with ice cubes and shake until the outside of the shaker feels icy cold. Strain into a martini glass (or 3 mini ones) garnish with coffee beans (if using) and serve at once.

Note: Bottled sugar syrup is available to buy but it's easy (and often convenient) to make your own at home. Simply combine 300 g/1½ cups caster/superfine or white granulated sugar in 150 ml/²⁄₃ cup cold water in a small heavy-based saucepan and set over a low heat. Cook for a few minutes, until the sugar has dissolved and the liquid thickened slightly.

Once cooled, your syrup will keep in a sterilized screw-top jar or bottle in the fridge for up to 4 weeks. This recipe will give you about 400 ml/1¾ cups of syrup. Use it as directed in any cocktail or party drink recipes in this book that requires sugar syrup.

CAMOMILE TEA & WHISKY TODDY

A whisky toddy is traditionally a cure-all for colds as well as a good night-time drink to help you sleep, but it makes the perfect winter pick-me-up any time of day.

2 lemons, plus extra juice to taste

6 cloves

2 camomile tea bags

400 ml/1½ cups just-boiled water

2 cinnamon sticks

a pinch of freshly grated nutmeg

1–3 tablespoons runny honey, plus extra to taste

90 ml/3 oz. Scotch whisky

SERVES 2

Cut half a lemon into slices and stud the skin of each slice with the cloves. Put the tea bags, hot water, cinnamon, nutmeg and lemon slices in a saucepan and simmer for 2–3 minutes.

Meanwhile, squeeze the juice from the remaining lemons. Take the tea off the heat and add the lemon juice, honey and whisky. Taste and add more lemon or honey if desired.

Strain the tea into 2 heatproof glasses or cups and drop a lemon slice and cinnamon stick into each glass. Give it one final stir with the cinnamon stick and serve at once.

CHILLI CHAI

Masala chai is essentially black tea infused with spices and served with lots of sweetened warm milk. There are infinite variations, and this recipe should only be regarded as a starting point. Enjoy playing around with the recipe to come up with your own perfect blend. Also, once you have your own signature spice blend, mix up a large batch and scoop into screw-top jars for great homemade gifts. Allowing the milk to reach boiling point is an integral part of making authentic chai, even though it seems to go against everything we were ever taught about heating milk!

2–3-cm/1-inch piece of fresh ginger root, finely sliced

2 star anise

1 fresh or dried bay leaf

8 cardamom pods, bruised

6 whole cloves

3-cm/1¼-inch piece of cinnamon stick

2.5-cm/1-inch piece of vanilla pod/bean

1 whole dried chilli/chile

250 ml/1 cup milk

1½ tablespoons runny honey

1 tablespoon loose black tea leaves, or 2 strong teabags

SERVES 2

Put 500 ml/2 cups cold water into a small, heavy-based saucepan and add the ginger, star anise, bay leaf, cardamom, cloves, cinnamon, vanilla and dried chilli/chile. Bring to the boil, then turn the heat down to achieve a gentle simmer. Simmer for about 10 minutes to allow the spices to infuse the water.

Add the milk and honey to the pan and bring to the boil for a brief moment before turning down the heat again to a gentle simmer.

Add the tea and simmer for 2 minutes before removing from the heat. Let stand for a further 2 minutes before straining into cups or heatproof glasses through a tea strainer and serve at once.

FRESH MINT GREEN TEA

The North African way is to pour this tea from a great height, creating bubbles on the surface of the drink. It is traditionally drunk in small, often decorative, tea glasses that are frequently replenished, and accompanied by delicious, sticky-sweet pastries. It aids digestion so is perfect enjoyed after a heavy meal.

4 teaspoons Chinese green tea, such as gunpowder

2 sprigs of fresh mint, ideally spearmint

500 ml/2 cups just-boiled water

½–2 teaspoons caster/superfine or white granulated sugar, to taste

a small handful of pine nuts (optional)

SERVES 2

Rinse a teapot with boiling water to warm it. Add the green tea and mint. Pour in the water and let infuse for 3 minutes.

Strain into 2 heatproof glasses or cups then stir in sugar, to taste. Put the pine nuts in the glasses, if using and serve at once. They soften as they soak and can be eaten at the end of the drink so remember to offer teaspoons alongside if you do include them.

MANUKA HONEY TEA

Manuka honey is a wonderful product with lots of health-giving properties, especially as a defence against winter colds and it makes a good sweetener in green tea. Simply make a pot of green tea and sweeten with manuka honey to taste, but let the water cool slightly first, as boiling water is thought to destroy some of the benefits.

3–4 teaspoons green tea leaves

500 ml/2 cups just-boiled water

manuka honey, to taste

SERVES 2

Rinse a teapot with boiling water to warm it. Add the tea leaves and pour over the just-boiled water. Leave to brew for 3–4 minutes. Pour into 2 cups or heatproof glasses, sweeten to taste with manuka honey and serve at once.

MATCHA TEA SOY LATTE

This delicious and unusual drink uses the fragrant, leafy taste of matcha green tea powder in a make-at-home version of a Japanese classic, the matcha latte.

2 teaspoons matcha green tea powder, plus extra to dust

2 teaspoons sugar, plus extra to serve

6 tablespoons warm water

500 ml/2 cups soya/soy milk (or dairy if preferred)

SERVES 2

Spoon the matcha green tea powder and sugar into a medium jug/pitcher. Add the water and mix with a spoon until it is smooth and lump-free.

Warm the milk in a small saucepan set over a medium heat and then pour it into the jug/pitcher. Use a balloon whisk to vigorously mix the paste and milk together until smooth with a light foam on top. Pour into 2 heatproof glasses or cups and add a dusting of matcha green tea powder to each one. Serve at once.

CINNAMON-SCENTED BLACK TEA

The main difference between black tea and other types is the greater oxidation of the leaves; this means that black teas hold their flavour for much longer, and are often mixed with strong spices and flavourings. Here, a robust Yunnan black tea is very simply infused with a cinnamon stick for a lightly spiced drink.

2 scoops black Yunnan tea leaves
cinnamon sticks
500 ml/2 cups just-boiled water
sugar or runny honey, to taste

2 stainless steel tea balls

SERVES 2

Place a scoop of black tea in each tea ball and place each in a tall cup or heatproof glass, along with a cinnamon stick.

Pour over just-boiled water and leave to infuse for 3 minutes. Sweeten with the tiniest amount of sugar or honey, which helps balance the cinnamon flavour. Serve at once.

GINGER & HONEY TEA

Ginger fans will love this tea – there's enough flavour from the fresh ginger to create a zingy, refreshing drink without actually adding tea leaves in any form, but you may prefer the additional depth a little green tea adds.

4 green tea bags, or the equivalent in green tea leaves if preferred

a 5-cm/2-inch piece of fresh ginger root, sliced

500 ml/2 cups just-boiled water

acacia honey, or similar light, flowery honey, to taste

SERVES 2

Rinse a teapot with boiling water to warm it. Add the green tea and ginger. Fill the teapot with the just-boiled water. Give everything a gentle stir and leave to infuse for 4–5 minutes.

Pour into cups or heatproof glasses, sweeten to taste with acacia honey and serve at once.

HOT HONEY LEMON TEA

If you order a cup of tea in Italy you will get a hot lemon tea – adding milk is considered rather eccentric! Why not try this for a refreshing change.

1 lemon

2 tablespoons runny honey

500 ml/2 cups freshly brewed black tea of your choice

SERVES 2

Cut 2 slices off the lemon and squeeze the juice from the rest. Divide the honey between 2 large heatproof glasses or cups, add a lemon slice and half the lemon juice to each, then top up with hot tea. Stir as the honey melts and serve at once.

RESTORATIVE

revivers, mulls & soothers

MORNING GLORY FIZZ

This drink originated in the late 1800s and was likely designed as a hangover cure. The silky smooth texture will soothe your 'morning after' headache and provide an easy-to-drink 'hair of the dog that bit you'... a very useful recipe to have up your sleeve during the party season...

60 ml/2 oz. Chivas Regal 12 Year Old Blended Scotch, or whisky of your choice

2½ teaspoons freshly squeezed lemon juice

2½ teaspoons freshly squeezed lime juice

20 ml/¾ oz. Simple Sugar Syrup (see page 62)

1 dash of absinthe (French aniseed flavoured spirit)

15 ml/½ oz. very fresh egg white

soda water, to top up

ice cubes

SERVES 1

Combine the whisky, lemon juice, lime juice, sugar syrup, absinthe and egg white in a cocktail shaker with a scoop of ice cubes and shake very hard for at least 30 seconds.

Strain into a flute glass (or small highball glass if preferred) without ice and top up with the soda water, creating a foamy head on the surface of the drink. Serve at once.

MULLED WINE

———◦◦◦◦◦———

2 clementines

1 lime

2 lemons

2 x 75-cl bottles fruity red wine

100 ml/⅓ cup brandy

200 g/1 cup caster/superfine
or white granulated sugar

1 cinnamon stick

4 cloves

4 pinches of freshly grated nutmeg

1 split vanilla pod/bean

extra cinnamon sticks, to garnish
(optional)

SERVES 10

Perhaps the most popular of all seasonal drinks,
a glass of spicy and aromatic mulled wine is
always welcome, and ideal for social gatherings.

Pare the peels from the clementines, lime and lemons
with a vegetable peeler and put it in a large saucepan,
reserving half of the lemon peels to garnish. Add the
freshly squeezed juice of the clementines to the pan,
along with the wine, brandy, sugar, cinnamon, cloves,
nutmeg and vanilla pod/bean. Set over a medium heat
and simmer gently, for 30 minutes, stirring occasionally.

Sieve/strain and ladle or pour into heatproof glasses
or punch cups. Garnish each one with a reserved lemon
zest and a cinnamon stick, if using, and serve at once.

MULLED BLOODY MARY

———◦◦◦◦◦———

1 litre/4 cups good-quality
tomato juice

1 lemon

1–2 tablespoons Worcestershire
sauce, to taste

salt and ground black pepper,
to season

80–125 ml/⅓–½ cup vodka

a pinch of celery salt

SERVES 4–6

This classic brunch cocktail is surprisingly tasty
when served hot so give it a try.

Put the tomato juice in a large saucepan. Cut half of
the lemon into slices and squeeze the juice from the
remaining half into the pan. Add the lemon slices and
Worcestershire sauce to the pan and season to taste.
Bring to the boil and simmer, uncovered, for 10 minutes.

Remove the saucepan from the heat and let cool for
about 20 minutes. Stir in the vodka and add celery salt
to taste. Serve at once in heatproof highball glasses.

HOT APPLE CIDER
WITH SLOE GIN

A cold, crisp day calls for a warm stiff drink and a hot apple cider is just the tipple for a warming pit-stop. If you have a juicer then try making your own cloudy apple juice/soft apple cider. With its perfect blend of autumn/fall fruits, heady spices and optional sloe gin, this really is all things nice.

400 ml/1¾ cups dry cider/ hard apple cider

100 ml/scant ½ cup cloudy apple juice/soft apple cider

3 cloves

2 cinnamon sticks

1 orange, sliced

30 ml/1 oz. sloe gin (optional)

demerara/turbinado sugar, to taste (optional)

SERVES 4

Put the cider/hard apple cider, apple juice/soft apple cider, cloves and cinnamon sticks into a large saucepan and slowly bring to a simmer over medium heat.

Turn off the heat as soon as it starts to bubble, then add the orange slices and sloe gin, if using. Add a little sugar, if it needs it, then pour into heatproof glasses or punch cups and serve at once.

HARVEST PUNCH

1 litre/4 cups dry cider/
hard apple cider

300 g/1½ cups demerara/
turbinado sugar

150 ml/⅔ cup Calvados (optional)

1 teaspoon allspice

1 teaspoon freshly ground nutmeg

1 teaspoon ground cinnamon

fresh apple slices studded
with cloves, to garnish

SERVES 6

This delicious winter warmer has plenty of bite to keep out the cold, even without the optional Calvados, a fortifying apple brandy from Spain.

Add the cider/hard apple cider, sugar, Calvados (if using), allspice, nutmeg and cinnamon to a large saucepan set over a medium heat and simmer gently for about 1 hour, stirring frequently.

Remove from the heat and pour into a punch bowl. Ladle into heatproof glasses or punch cups, garnished with the clove-studded apple slices and serve at once.

HOT RUM & CIDER PUNCH

500 ml/2 cups dry cider/
hard apple cider

2 lemon slices

1 apple, cored and thinly sliced

1 cinnamon stick, crushed

3 cloves

2 tablespoons demerara/
turbinado sugar

75 ml/⅓ cup dark rum

SERVES 4–6

Apple slices infused with cider, dark rum and spices make this a great drink for a Halloween party. To serve a non-alcoholic version, replace the cider/hard apple cider with juice and omit the rum.

Put the cider/hard apple cider, lemon slices, apple slices, cinnamon, cloves, sugar and rum in a large saucepan and heat the mixture gently until it just reaches boiling point.

Simmer gently for 10 minutes, then remove from the heat and let infuse for 10 minutes. Sieve/strain, ladle into heatproof glasses or punch cups and serve at once.

PORTUGUESE MULLED PORT

Similar to mulled wine (see page 80) but made using port, this is an elegant spiced punch perfect for a winter dinner party. It is fairly potent though so serve it in small demitasse cups (or heatproof glasses) at the end of a meal.

2 oranges

10 cloves

6 allspice berries

1 cinnamon stick

¼ teaspoon freshly grated
  nutmeg

50 g/¼ cup demerara/
  turbinado sugar

75-cl bottle ruby port

a pestle and mortar

SERVES 12

Peel and slice 1 orange and squeeze the juice from the second orange. Put the slices and freshly squeezed juice in a large saucepan and pour in 480 ml/2 scant cups of cold water.

Lightly crush the cloves, allspice and cinnamon in a pestle and mortar and add to the pan, along with the nutmeg. Add the sugar and bring the mixture slowly to the boil, stirring until the sugar has dissolved.

Simmer gently for 10 minutes. Stir in the port and heat gently, without boiling, for a further 2–3 minutes. Sieve/strain and pour into small heatproof glasses or punch cups and serve at once.

CLASSIC HOT TODDY

For some reason this drink is often only consumed when the drinker feels under the weather, but the hot toddy is a great everyday winter warmer. It's perfect for sipping after any outdoor activity when things have turned frosty.

1 tablespoon runny honey

50 ml/2 oz. Scotch whisky

25 ml/1 oz. freshly squeezed lemon juice

a pinch of ground cinnamon or 1 cinnamon stick

just-boiled water, to top up

2 lemon zests, studded with cloves, to garnish

SERVES 1

Add the honey, whisky, lemon juice and cinnamon to a heatproof glass and stir gently with a spoon to mix.

Top up the glass with just-boiled water, stir to dissolve the honey and garnish with the lemon zests studded with cloves. Serve at once.

NEGUS

There always seems to be plenty of port around during the festive season, and rightly so. You could happily while away the hours after dinner, passing the bottle to your left but if you're looking for a different way to enjoy it, try this recipe or the Portuguese Mulled Port on page 87.

75 ml/2½ oz. Tawny port

30 ml/1 oz. freshly squeezed lemon juice

10 ml/⅓ oz. Simple Sugar Syrup (see page 62)

just-boiled water, to top up

a lemon zest, to garnish

freshly grated nutmeg, to serve

SERVES 1

Add the port, lemon juice and sugar syrup to a heatproof glass or cup and stir gently with a spoon to mix.

Top up with boiling water, garnish with a lemon zest and a dusting of grated nutmeg. Serve at once.

HOT BUTTERED RUM

3 teaspoons demerara/
turbinado sugar

60 ml/2 oz. dark rum

½ teaspoon allspice

1 teaspoon butter

just-boiled water, to top up

an orange zest studded with
cloves, to garnish

SERVES 1

White rum may be the perfect ingredient for
a summer Carribean-style cocktail, but dark rum
happily lends itself to drinks just made for winter
nights, especially once combined with warming
spices and sweetened with brown sugar, as here.

Warm a heatproof glass or cup and add the sugar and a
little just-boiled water. Stir until the sugar has dissolved
and then add the rum, allspice and butter. Top up with
more hot water and stir until the butter has melted.

Garnish with a piece of orange zest studded with cloves,
and serve at once.

CINNAMON BUTTERED RUM

25 g/1½ tablespoons butter

2 tablespoons demerara/
turbinado sugar

1 cinnamon stick

200 ml/¾ cup Captain Morgan's
Spiced, or other spiced gold rum

extra cinnamon sticks, to garnish
(optional)

SERVES 4

The traditional recipe for buttered rum is diluted
with water, but here it's served neat in a smaller
glass and made with a gold rum, that has been
flavoured with warming spices, including cinnamon.

Gently heat the butter, sugar and cinnamon stick in
a saucepan, until the butter has melted and the sugar
dissolved. Stir in the rum and gently heat through. Discard
the cinnamon and pour the drink into small heatproof
glasses or cups, garnish each one with a half a cinnamon
stick, if using, and serve at once.

APPLE PIE MOONSHINE

You can use either a bottled apple pie moonshine here or homemade, if you have it. It packs quite a punch so is really best enjoyed as a diluted ingredient in a cocktail. These cute mini-size servings work well served with small bites at a party.

120 ml/4 oz. apple pie moonshine (such as Midnight Moon)

120 ml/4 oz. cloudy apple juice/ soft apple cider

50 ml/1²/₃ oz. cinnamon syrup (such as Monin)

30 ml/1 oz. freshly squeezed lemon juice

small green and/or red apple wedges, to garnish

ice cubes

SERVES 4

Pour the apple pie moonshine, apple juice/soft apple cider, cinnamon syrup and lemon juice into a cocktail shaker filled with ice cubes and shake until frosted.

Pour the drink into shot glasses or mini tankards (as pictured) and garnish each one with an apple wedge. Serve at once.

SAZERAC

—◆◇◆—

The sazerac cocktail hails back to the mid-1800s and is said to have been created at the Sazerac Coffee House in New Orleans. The original sazerac cocktail was probably made with brandy, but has since evolved to more commonly use rye whiskey, as here. Either way, it makes the perfect warming soother to sip while curled up with a good book by the fireside.

5 ml/1 teaspoon absinthe (French aniseed spirit)

60 ml/2 oz. Sazerac Rye Whiskey, or rye whiskey of your choice

5 ml/1 teaspoon Simple Sugar Syrup (see page 62)

3 dashes of Peychaud's Bitters

a large strip of lemon zest, to season

crushed ice and ice cubes

SERVES 1

Add the absinthe to a small rocks glass filled with crushed ice and leave the glass to chill while preparing the drink.

Combine the rye whiskey, sugar syrup and bitters in a mixing glass with a scoop of ice cubes and stir for about 30 seconds.

Discard the crushed ice and absinthe from the rocks glass before straining the drink into the chilled, absinthe-rinsed rocks glass. Squeeze the lemon zest to express the citrus oils over the top and sides of the glass and discard the zest. Serve at once.

OLD FASHIONED

One of the most popular cocktails of all time, this drink is likely the 'original cocktail' – in the sense that the oldest recorded recipe we have for a cocktail lists the ingredients as a base spirit, bitters, sugar and water (or ice). It has come back in vogue in recent years, thanks to vintage-style popular culture influences such as the *Mad Men* TV series and makes the perfect winter soother.

7.5 ml/1½ teaspoons Simple Sugar Syrup (see page 62)

3 dashes of Angostura bitters

60 ml/2 oz. Michter's Bourbon, or bourbon of your choice

a large strip of orange zest, to season and garnish

ice cubes

SERVES 1

Combine the sugar syrup, Angostura bitters and bourbon in a mixing glass and add a large scoop of ice cubes. Stir for 20–30 seconds.

Strain into a rocks glass filled with ice cubes. Squeeze the orange zest over the top of the drink to express the citrus oils, then drop it into the glass to garnish. Serve at once.

WHISKEY SOUR

Along with the Old Fashioned (see page 99) and Manhattan (see Sparkling Manhattan page 117), the Whiskey Sour is another quintessential American whiskey cocktail. The combination of bourbon, lemon juice, sugar syrup, bitters and egg white is unbeatable, and the reason this drink remains so popular in bars around the world today but you can enjoy it at home too.

50 ml/1²/₃ oz. Woodford Reserve Bourbon, or bourbon of your choice

25 ml/³/₄ oz. freshly squeezed lemon juice

25 ml/³/₄ oz. Simple Sugar Syrup (see page 62)

20 ml/³/₄ oz. very fresh egg white

3 dashes of Angostura bitters, plus extra to garnish

a lemon slice and maraschino cherry, to garnish

ice cubes

SERVES 1

Combine the bourbon, lemon juice, sugar syrup, egg white and Angostura butters in a cocktail shaker and 'dry' shake first (i.e. with no ice) just to emulsify the egg white.

Add a scoop of ice cubes to the cocktail shaker and shake vigorously. Strain into a rocks glass filled with ice cubes and garnish with the lemon slice, maraschino cherry and an extra dash of Angostura bitters. Serve at once.

PENICILLIN

The smokiness of the Scotch whisky combines perfectly with lemon, honey and ginger to make the ultimate sore throat soother and warmer. The Honey Ginger Syrup can also be used to make mocktails; simply put a few tablespoons of it in an ice cube filled glass and top up with cloudy lemonade or, for a toddy, spoon into a heatproof glass and top up with hot water and a squeeze of lemon juice.

50 ml/1²/₃ oz. Chivas Regal 12 Year Old Blended Scotch, or blended Scotch whisky of your choice

10 ml/2 teaspoons Laphroaig 10 Year Old Single Malt Scotch, or single malt Scotch whisky of your choice

25 ml/¾ oz. freshly squeezed lemon juice

25 ml/¾ oz. Honey Ginger Syrup (see below)

stem/candied ginger and lemon wedge, to garnish

ice cubes

FOR THE HONEY GINGER SYRUP

250 ml/¾ cup runny honey

15-cm/6-inch piece of fresh ginger root, peeled and sliced

SERVES 1

Combine the 2 Scotches, lemon juice and honey ginger syrup in a cocktail shaker. Add a scoop of ice cubes and shake hard. Strain into a rocks glass filled with ice cubes. Garnish with stem/candied ginger and a lemon wedge.

To make Honey Ginger Syrup, put the honey and ginger in a saucepan, add 250 ml/1 cup cold water and stir to mix. Bring to the boil, reduce the heat and simmer for 5 minutes. Let the syrup cool then remove the solids using a fine-mesh sieve/strainer and discard.

Store the syrup in a sealed sterilized bottle or screw-top jar in the fridge and use within 1 month.

BOBBY BURNS

This twist on the Rob Roy was named after Scottish poet Robert Burns. To add extra depth to the drink, try including a dash of absinthe and/or orange bitters. The smokiness of the Scotch works perfectly with the herbaceous and spicy notes of the Benedictine in this warming cocktail making it perfect for the colder months.

50 ml/1⅔ oz. Glenmorangie The Original Single Malt Scotch Whisky, or single malt Scotch whisky of your choice

25 ml/¾ oz. Martini Rosso, or other sweet red vermouth

2½ teaspoons Benedictine (French herbal liqueur)

lemon zest, to season and garnish

ice cubes

SERVES 1

Combine the whisky, vermouth and Benedictine in a mixing glass with a scoop of ice cubes.

Stir for about 30 seconds before straining into a chilled coupette or cocktail glass. Squeeze the lemon zest to express the citrus oils over the drink before using it to garnish the glass. Serve at once.

IRISH FLIP

Here we have an Irish take on the classic flip recipe. Flips were originally enjoyed hot, but this creamy drink works equally well when served cold. Similar to eggnog, it includes a delicious syrup made by slowly reducing a dark dry stout. It's a good, nourishing drink to serve during the winter months.

50 ml/1²⁄₃ oz. Jameson Irish Whiskey, or Irish whiskey of your choice

25 ml/¾ oz. Dark Stout Syrup (see below)

1 whole egg

2 teaspoons Pedro Ximénez sherry

freshly grated nutmeg, to garnish

FOR THE DARK STOUT SYRUP

500 ml/2 cups dark Irish stout (such as Guinness)

250 ml/1 cup demerara/ turbinado sugar

ice cubes

SERVES 1

Add the whiskey, Dark Stout Syrup, egg and sherry to a cocktail shaker with a scoop of ice cubes and shake hard. Strain into a small wine glass. Garnish with grated nutmeg and serve at once.

To make the Dark Stout Syrup, put the stout in a saucepan and simmer over a medium heat for 30–40 minutes until the volume is reduced by half. Add the sugar and stir until dissolved. Remove from the heat and allow to cool.

Store the syrup in a sealed sterilized bottle or screw-top jar in the fridge and use within 1 month.

BABY BRANDY ALEXANDER

---

60 ml/2 oz. Cognac

30 ml/1 oz. dark crème de cacao (chocolate liqueur)

30 ml/1 oz. single/light cream

freshly grated nutmeg, to garnish

ice cubes

SERVES 2

Here is a classic rich and creamy cocktail that particularly benefits from being served in a small portion. Serve it as an elegant (and easy to prepare) pre-dessert at a festive dinner or as an alternative to a welcoming eggnog.

Put the brandy, crème de cacao and cream into a cocktail shaker filled with ice cubes. Shake vigorously until the shaker frosts.

Pour into small cocktail or dessert wine glasses and garnish with freshly grated nutmeg. Serve at once.

CHOC MINT ALEXANDER

---

45 ml/1¾ oz. Cognac

10 ml/⅓ oz. dark crème de cacao

10 ml/⅓ oz. white crème de cacao

10 ml/⅓ oz. crème de menthe

20 ml/¾ oz. single/light cream

15 ml/½ oz. very fresh egg white (optional)

1 dash of chocolate bitters

powdered drinking chocolate and a fresh mint leaf, to garnish

ice cubes

SERVES 1

A delicious, lip-tingling minty riff on the traditional Brandy Alexander. For a truly seasonal party drink, you can replace the fresh mint leaf and chocolate dusting with crumbled peppermint bark.

Put the brandy, dark crème de cacao, white crème de cacao, crème de menthe, cream and egg white (if using) into a cocktail shaker filled with ice cubes. Shake vigorously until the shaker frosts.

Pour into a coupe and garnish with a dusting of powdered drinking chocolate and a mint leaf. Serve at once.

CELEBRATORY

sparkling cocktails & party drinks

KIR ROYALE

The most classic of aperitifs, this elegantly bubbly cocktail is perfect
served at any smart winter occasion.

**15 ml/½ oz. crème de cassis
(blackcurrant liqueur)**

well-chilled Champagne, to top up

**a fresh or frozen blackberry,
to garnish (optional)**

SERVES 1

Put the cassis in a flute glass and drop in the blackberry,
if using. Pour in a little of the chilled Champagne, allow
it to fizz up then settle before topping up. Serve at once.

CHAMBORD ROYALE

This subtle twist on the Kir Royale (above) uses a black raspberry liqueur, rather
than the traditional crème de cassis and combines it with sparkling Crémant,
a delicious and more affordable alternative to Champagne.

**15 ml/½ oz. Chambord
(black raspberry liqueur)**

well-chilled Crémant, to top up

**a lemon zest twist, to garnish
(optional)**

SERVES 1

Put the Chambord in a flute glass. Pour in a little of the
Crémant, allow it to fizz up then settle before topping up.

Garnish with a lemon zest twist, if using, and serve at once.

CRANBERRY & ORANGE SPARKLER

— ◦◦◦ —

This is the ideal companion to a festive brunch party. It's light, refreshing and if you use an Italian Rosé Vino Frizzante, it will be a little lower in alcohol than a Prosecco or Champagne-based cocktail, so perfect for drinking before midday!

10 ml/⅓ oz. Cointreau (orange-flavoured liqueur)

40 ml/1½ oz. well-chilled cranberry juice

75–100 ml/2½–3⅓ oz. well-chilled lightly sparkling rosé wine

orange zest twist and/or fresh cranberries, to garnish

SERVES 1

Pour the Cointreau and cranberry juice into a flute glass and slowly top up with the chilled sparkling rosé wine.

Garnish with an orange zest twist and/or a few fresh cranberries on a cocktail stick/toothpick. Serve at once.

SPARKLING MANHATTAN

If you love a Manhattan but sometimes find them a bit strong, you'll love this. It is based on a Sweet Manhattan, but feel free to switch the sweet vermouth for dry if you prefer yours dry. If you want a non-alcoholic option to pair well with this drink at a party, try the Berry Apple Fizz on page 121.

15 ml/½ oz. bourbon

10 ml/⅓ oz. sweet red vermouth

a dash of Angostura bitters

5 ml/1 teaspoon Maraschino, such as Luxardo

well-chilled Champagne or other dry sparkling wine, to top up

3 maraschino cherries threaded onto a cocktail stick/toothpIck, to garnish

ice cubes

SERVES 1

Pour the bourbon, vermouth, Angostura bitters and Maraschino into a cocktail shaker filled with ice and stir well.

Strain into an old-fashioned glass filled with ice cubes and top up with the chilled Champagne. Garnish with the maraschino cherries and serve at once.

CRANBERRY CASSIS

40 ml/1½ oz. cranberry juice

15 ml/½ oz. crème de cassis

well-chilled Cava, to top up

a sprig of redcurrants, to garnish (optional)

ice cubes

SERVES 1

This slightly drier and fruitier twist on a Kir Royale (see page 113) would be perfect for a festive gathering. The crimson cranberry juice adds a little special Christmas magic, but it's refreshing and light at any time of year.

Pour the cranberry juice and crème de cassis into a cocktail shaker filled with ice cubes and shake well. Strain into a chilled flute glass or small wine glass and top up with the chilled Cava. Garnish with the redcurrants, if using, and serve.

ORANGE & CRANBERRY SPARKLE

250 ml/1 cup fresh orange juice

250 ml/1 cup cranberry juice

250 ml/1 cup sparkling elderflower drink, such as Bottle Green's Elderflower Pressé

orange zests and fresh cranberries, to garnish

ice cubes

SERVES 4

This tangy fizz gets it's bubbles from sparkling elderflower. It is pretty to look at, refreshing to drink and makes a great choice as a non-alcoholic option for a party, as it is simplicity itself to make.

Make sure all of the ingredients are well chilled.

Combine them in a jug/pitcher with some ice cubes and carefully pour into flute glasses.

Garnish each one with a few cranberries and an orange zest. Serve at once.

APPLE JACK

---

15 ml/½ oz. Calvados (Spanish apple brandy)

15 ml/½ oz. crème de cassis (blackcurrant liqueur)

well-chilled Crémant or Cava, to top up

ice cubes

SERVES 1

Slightly more potent than other sparkling cocktails, due to the addition of Calvados, this is the perfect choice to get your party started!

Pour the Calvados and crème de cassis into a cocktail shaker filled with ice cubes and stir. Strain into a chilled flute glass, top up with the chilled Crémant or Cava and serve at once.

BERRY APPLE FIZZ

---

15 ml/½ oz. Red Berry & Cinnamon Syrup (see below)

75 ml/2½ oz. unsweetened cloudy apple juice/soft apple cider

well-chilled soda, to top up

a few fresh raspberries threaded onto a cocktail stick/toothpick and a green apple slice, to garnish

crushed ice

FOR THE RED BERRY & CINNAMON SYRUP

340 g/12 oz. mixed frozen berries

150 g/¾ cup caster/white granulated sugar

2 cinnamon sticks

SERVES 1

This attractive mocktail combines a cinnamon-spiced red berry syrup with apple juice/soft apple cider and is served over crushed ice.

First make the Red Berry & Cinnamon Syrup (this will make a large batch and keep in a sterilized screw-top jar for up to 1 week if refrigerated). Combine the frozen berries and the sugar in a heavy-bottomed saucepan and add a splash of water and drop in the cinnamon sticks. Set over medium heat and bring to the boil, reduce to a simmer and cook until the berries have softened and the juice is syrupy. Force through a small sieve/strainer into a jug/pitcher. Discard the pulp and cinnamon sticks.

Half-fill a rocks glass with crushed ice. Add a spoonful of the Red Berry Syrup and the apple juice/soft apple cider. Top up with a splash of the chilled soda. Garnish with the raspberries and an apple slice. Serve at once.

PROSECCO WHITE LADY

The White Lady is a well-known 1920s classic and it's pale wintry elegance makes it a sophisticated choice for the cocktail hour. Here this legend is made even lovelier, thanks to a generous helping of sparkling chilled Prosecco.

40 ml/1½ oz. gin

15 ml/½ oz. Cointreau

15 ml/½ oz. freshly squeezed lemon juice

well-chilled Prosecco, to top up

ice cubes

SERVES 1

Pour the gin, Cointreau and lemon juice into a cocktail shaker half-filled with ice cubes. Stir until very cold, then strain into a chilled martini glass.

Top up with the chilled Prosecco and serve at once.

PROSECCO CLASSICO

If it's good enough for Champagne, it's good enough for Prosecco! Roll out the red carpet and give your Italian bubbles the classic cocktail treatment by serving it in this classic sparkling style.

a few dashes of Angostura bitters

1 sugar cube

a dash of brandy

150 ml/5 oz. well-chilled Prosecco

SERVES 1

Drop several dashes of Angostura bitters onto the sugar cube and drop it into a chilled flute glass. Add a dash of brandy, then fill the glass with chilled Prosecco and serve at once.

FESTIVE FIZZ

Fresh, fruity, fizzy and just the thing for adding seasonal sparkle
to your Christmas drinks party. Cheers!

½ fresh clementine, in segments

15 ml/½ oz. Cointreau

25 ml/1 oz. pomegranate juice

well-chilled Prosecco, to top up

fresh pomegranate seeds,
  to garnish

ice cubes

SERVES 1

Put the clementine segments into a cocktail shaker
with the Cointreau. Muddle (crush) well with a
muddler (or the end of a wooden rolling pin), then add
the pomegranate juice and a few ice cubes and shake.

Strain into a flute glass and add the pomegranate seeds
to garnish. Top up with the chilled Prosecco and serve
at once.

NIGHT OWL

Any night owl worth their salt, and even a few guests who should know better,
will enjoy this wickedly quaffable creation as the party warms up.

15 ml/½ oz. gin

15 ml/½ oz. crème de cassis

15 ml/½ oz. pomegranate juice

well-chilled Prosecco, to top up

a strip of lemon zest, to season
  and garnish

ice cubes

SERVES 1

Put the gin, crème de cassis and pomegranate juice in a
cocktail shaker half-filled with ice cubes and shake well.

Strain into a chilled martini glass and top up with the
chilled Prosecco. Squeeze the lemon zest strip in half
lengthways so that the essential oils in the skin spritz
on to the drink, then drop it in. Serve at once.

HIBISCUS FIZZ

Hibiscus flowers are said to have health benefits, but never mind all that, let's put some in Prosecco to impress your guests! The flowers preserved in syrup in a jar are widely available now, and add a lovely pink colour and sweet, fruity tang to your bubbles. This drink couldn't be easier or prettier.

1 hibiscus flower in syrup, from a jar

5 ml/1 teaspoon of syrup from the hibiscus flower jar, or grenadine

well-chilled Prosecco, to top up

SERVES 1

Carefully place the hibiscus flower with the petals facing upwards in the bottom of a chilled flute glass. Add the syrup, and slowly pour in the chilled Prosecco as you watch the flower unfurl. Serve at once.

SPARKLING HIBISCUS TEA FIZZ

Tea makes a good base for non-alcoholic cocktails, and cold-brewing the tea here rather than using hot water gives a smoother, more delicate taste. Top up with sparkling tonic water for an elegant festive fizz.

1 hibiscus teabag

runny honey or agave syrup, to taste

well-chilled, good-quality tonic water, to top up

dried hibiscus flowers, to garnish

SERVES 1

First make the cold-brew hibiscus tea. Put the teabag in a measuring jug/pitcher, add 175 ml/¾ cup of cold water and refrigerate for a few hours or overnight.

When ready to make the drink, add a spoonful of honey or agave syrup to the jug/pitcher and whisk into the tea. Pour half of the hibiscus tea into a chilled flute glass, top up with chilled tonic water and garnish with dried hibiscus flowers. Serve at once.

PROSECCO COSMOPOLITAN

Perhaps the best-known vodka cocktail, the fun and flirty Cosmopolitan gets a bubbly makeover here with the addition of some chilled fizz.

25 ml/1 oz. vodka

55 ml/2 oz. cranberry juice

5 ml/1 teaspoon freshly squeezed lime juice

well-chilled Prosecco, to top up

a strip of orange zest, to season and garnish

ice cubes

SERVES 1

Put the vodka, cranberry juice and lime juice in a cocktail shaker filled with ice cubes. Shake well and strain into a chilled martini glass. Top up with the chilled Prosecco.

Squeeze the orange zest strip in half lengthways so that the essential oils in the skin spritz on to the drink, then drop it in. Serve at once

PRIMA DONNA

This fruity cocktail is as pretty as it is delicious, thanks to the addition of bursting bubbles, more usually found in bubble tea, but available to buy for cocktails too.

1 teaspoon Popaball® Passionfruit Bursting Bubbles (optional)

25 ml/1 oz. vodka

15 ml/½ oz. limoncello (Italian lemon liqueur)

25 ml/1 oz. pomegranate juice

well-chilled Prosecco, to top up

ice cubes

SERVES 1

Add a spoonful of bursting passionfruit bubbles to a flute glass, if using. Put the vodka, limoncello and pomegranate juice in a cocktail shaker filled with ice cubes. Shake vigorously and strain into the glass.

Top up with the chilled Prosecco and serve at once.

ROSÉ, BOURBON & BLUE

The puréed fresh blueberries in this julep-style punch give the drink both its distinctive flavour and juicy body while the tannin from the tea is just detectable underneath the smoky notes of the bourbon. Deliciously reviving and the perfect drink to serve from your treasured Christmas/Holiday punch bowl.

100 g/½ cup raw cane sugar

250 g/2 cups fresh blueberries, rinsed and picked over for stems

500 ml/2 cups brewed unsweetened black tea, cooled

330 ml/1⅓ cups dry, fruity rosé wine (a Chilean Cabernet-blend works well here)

250 ml/1 cup bourbon

175 ml/¾ cup freshly squeezed lemon juice

lemon slices and blueberries, to garnish

ice cubes

SERVES 6–8

Stir the sugar with 7 tablespoons of hot water in a small bowl until the sugar is dissolved. Transfer to the cup of a blender. Add 125 g/1 cup of the blueberries to the processor and purée. Set a sieve/strainer over a large jug/pitcher. Strain the blueberry mixture, pressing on the solids with the back of a wooden spoon to extract as much liquid as possible. Discard the solids. Add the cooled tea, rosé, bourbon and lemon juice to the jug/pitcher. Cover and refrigerate until chilled, about 2 hours.

When ready to serve, add the remaining blueberries to the jug/pitcher and pour the drink into a punch bowl. Fill rocks glasses with ice cubes and divide the drink among the glasses.

Garnish each serving with a lemon slice and a blueberry. Serve at once.

WINTER GIN TONICA

A gin and tonic is not normally associated with the colder months, but there are some great wintery ways to serve it. This recipe uses a gin with pleasant, spiced notes and in addition to tonic, there is warming sparkling ginger ale, an optional ginger wine and a clove-studded garnish in the mix, too.

45 ml/1¾ oz. Warner Edwards Gin (other good choices include Portobello Gin and Edinburgh Gin)

75 ml/2½ oz. well-chilled good-quality tonic water

75 ml/2½ oz. well-chilled sparkling ginger ale

5 ml/1 teaspoon ginger wine or The King's Ginger Liqueur (optional)

ice cubes

TO GARNISH

an orange wedge studded with 3–4 cloves

extra cloves

a cinnamon stick

SERVES 1

Add fresh ice cubes to three-quarter fill a clean balloon glass (a Spanish copa is ideal). Stir gently for 15 seconds with a bar spoon or chopstick to chill the glass. Pour away any liquid from the melted ice. Top up the glass with more ice cubes.

Add the gin, trying to ensure that you coat the ice as you pour. Add the tonic water, ginger ale and ginger wine or liqueur, if using. Pouring slowly helps the tonic to keep its fizz.

Add the garnish. Let rest for 30 seconds to allow the flavours to integrate with each other, then serve.

NEW YEAR'S GIN TONICA

The end of another year deserves a special celebratory gin and tonic doesn't it? This bright and crisp drink is a great way to say goodbye to one year and welcome in the next. The drink uses Hammer & Son Old English Gin, which is lightly sweetened and has a full, spicy character. Even the bottle has a festive air, as the gin is packaged in old Champagne bottles. The Brut Champagne adds both extra fizz and a little dryness.

45 ml/1¾ oz. Hammer & Son Old English Gin, or similar style

200 ml/6¾ oz. well-chilled good-quality tonic water

45 ml/1¾ oz. Brut Champagne (or other dry sparkling wine)

3 dashes of orange bitters

a flamed orange zest, to season and garnish (see Note)

ice cubes

SERVES 1

Add fresh ice cubes to three-quarter fill a clean balloon glass (a Spanish copa is ideal). Stir gently for 15 seconds with a bar spoon or chopstick to chill the glass. Pour away any liquid from the melted ice. Top up the glass with more ice cubes.

Add the gin, trying to ensure that you coat the ice as you pour. Add the tonic water (pouring slowly helps it keep its fizz), then the Champagne and orange bitters.

Add the flamed orange peel garnish (see below). Let rest for 30 seconds to allow the flavours to integrate with each other. Serve.

Note: To make a flamed orange zest, take a washed, firm-skinned orange and use a sharp knife or vegetable peeler to cut an ample strip of peel, taking care to avoid the flesh. Strike a long match and wait a moment for the sulphur from the match head to burn away. (Lighter fluid can affect taste so stick to matches.) Hold the flame near the drink's surface. With the skin-side of the orange facing toward the flame, quickly press your thumb and index fingers toward each other. The citrus oils from the orange will be expelled, ignited, and land in the drink. Use the peel to garnish the drink.

SANTA'S LITTLE HELPER

Forget the glass of milk and cookies – this is what Santa *really* wants
to find when he/she calls at your home this holiday season.

20 ml/¾ oz. Pedro Ximenez sherry

15 ml/½ oz. ginger wine

15 ml/½ oz. fresh orange juice

well-chilled Prosecco, to top up

a strip of orange zest, to season and garnish

ice cubes

SERVES 1

Put the sherry, ginger wine and orange juice in a cocktail shaker and add a handful of ice cubes. Shake well and strain into a chilled flute glass.

Top up with the chilled Prosecco. Squeeze the orange zest strip in half lengthways so that the essential oils in the skin spritz on to the drink, then drop it in. Serve at once.

ST CLEMENT'S FIZZ

This zesty creation does sing of oranges and lemons and makes
a fabulously refreshing winter aperitif.

10 ml/⅓ oz. Cointreau

10 ml/⅓ oz. limoncello (Italian lemon liqueur)

10 ml/⅓ oz. Aperol

a dash of orange bitters

well-chilled Prosecco, to top up

lemon and orange zests, to garnish

ice cubes

SERVES 1

Pour the Cointreau, limoncello and Aperol into a cocktail shaker filled with ice cubes and add the orange bitters.

Stir well, strain into a flute glass and top with the chilled Prosecco. Garnish with orange and lemon zests and serve at once.

FIRESIDE SANGRIA

Who said rosé wine was just for summer? Here is a delicious sparkling wine punch to cosy up with on colder days. It makes a lighter and refreshing alternative to Mulled Wine (see page 80).

about 10 seedless white grapes, halved lengthways

about 10 seedless red grapes, halved lengthways

1 small orange, finely sliced

90 ml/3 oz. Grand Marnier or other orange-flavoured liqueur

90 ml/3 oz. aged sweet red vermouth (such as Carpano Antica Formula)

170 ml/¾ cup fresh clementine or blood orange juice

375 ml/1½ cups well-chilled fresh, fruity Sauvignon Blanc (preferably from New Zealand)

75-cl bottle well-chilled sparkling rosé (a pink Prosecco or Cava works well here)

dried orange slices and cinnamon sticks, to garnish

ice cubes

SERVES 6–8

Put the grapes and orange slices in a punch bowl or a large jug/pitcher, as preferred.

Pour in the Grand Marnier, vermouth, clementine or blood orange juice, white wine and rosé wine and stir to combine. Add plenty of ice cubes and stir again.

Serve ladled into tumblers or short-stemmed wine glasses filled with ice cubes and garnish each one with a dried orange slice and a cinnamon stick. Serve at once.

SWEDISH GLÖGG

Glögg translates as ember and this is the ultimate fireside drink for lovers of anything mulled. It is a punch and not practical to make in small quantities so this recipe will make about 20 small servings, perfect for creating a little 'hygge' by serving it with a cheesy bite after a festive meal instead of port.

peel of 1 small orange,
** ideally in 1 piece**

75-cl bottle fruity red wine

355 ml/1½ cups ruby port

250 ml/1 cup brandy

2 tablespoons light brown sugar

1 tablespoon whole cardamom
** pods, crushed**

6 cloves

1 cinnamon stick

small raisins and slivered/
** sliced almonds, to serve**

flamed orange zests, to garnish
** (optional), see Note on page 134**

SERVES 20

Using metal tongs, hold the orange peel over a flame on the hob/cooktop until it spots brown. Drop it into a large saucepan.

Add the wine, port, brandy, sugar and spices. Simmer, uncovered, over a medium heat for about 20 minutes then strain into a heatproof jug/pitcher.

Pour into small heatproof glasses or tankards. Add a few raisins and almond slivers to each serving and garnish with a flamed orange zest, if using. Offer small spoons for your guests to fish out the raisins and eat them. Serve at once.

RECIPE CREDITS

LOUISE PICKFORD
Honeyed Milk with Raisins
Babyccino
Caribbean Café with Rum
    & Malibu
Catalan Coffee Punch
Eggnog Latte
Golden Saffron Milk
Mochaccino
Portuguese Mulled Port
Rosemary Milk
Spiced Chilli Coconut Milk
Vanilla & Maple Soyaccino
Vanilla Coffee
White Christmas
Camomile Tea & Whisky
    Toddy
Mulled Bloody Mary
Hot Honey Tea
Hot Rum & Cider Punch

HANNAH MILES
Chai-Spiced White Hot
    Chocolate
Chilli Hot Chocolate
Cinnamon & Clementine
    Hot Chocolate
Gingerbread Hot Chocolate

Hazelnut Hot Chocolate
Pumpkin Spice Latte
S'mores Hot Chocolate
Toffee Apple Hot Chocolate

JULIA CHARLES
Introduction
Apple Pie Moonshine
Baby Brandy Alexander
Berry Apple Fizz
Chambord Royale
Choc Mint Alexander
Cinnamon Buttered Rum
Cinnamon Coffee
Cranberry & Orange Sparkler
Espresso Martini
Fireside Sangria
Kir Royale
Matcha Tea Soy Latte
Orange & Cranberry Sparkle
Rose, Bourbon & Blue
Sparkling Hibiscus Tea Fizz
Swedish Glögg

LAURA GLADWIN
Apple Jack
Cranberry Cassis
Festive Fizz

Hibiscus Fizz
Night Owl
Prima Donna
Prosecco Classico
Prosecco Cosmopolitan
Prosecco White Lady
Santa's Little Helper
Sparkling Manhattan
St Clement's Fizz

JESSE ESTES
Bobby Burns
Irish Flip
Morning Glory Fizz
Old Fashioned
Penicillin
Sazerac
Whiskey Sour

BEN REED
Classic Hot Toddy
Harvest Punch
Hot Buttered Rum
Mulled Wine
Negus

LIZ FRANKLIN
Cinnamon-Scented Black Tea

Fresh Mint Green Tea
Ginger & Honey Tea
Manuka Honey Tea

JASON CLARK
(adapted recipes, extracted
from Jason Clark's *The Art
& Craft of Coffee Cocktails*)
Campfire Mocha
Dutch Coffee
Irish Coffee

DAVID T. SMITH
New Year's Gin Tonica
Winter Gin Tonica

CLAIRE BURNET
Indulgent Hot Chocolate

LINDA COLLISTER
Mocha Maple Coffee

TORI FINCH
Hot Apple Cider with
    Sloe Gin

DAN MAY
Chilli Chai

PICTURE CREDITS